Conchas y Café Zine
Vol. IX, Issue 1

Buried Seeds
Grow

a  publication

DSTL Arts presents

Buried Seeds Grow
Conchas y Café Zine
Vol. IX, Issue 1

Cover and Book Design: Abraham Jaramillo

ISBN: 978-1-946081-72-8

10 9 8 7 6 5 4 3 2 1

www.DSTLArts.org

Los Angeles, CA

Contents

No Time Left

Mojdeh Amini

To breathe
Must run as roots

No time left

To be
Must live as lions

No time left
Must run

Must live

Not Mine

Sanjui

Not mine, not yours
And who decides
For is this the promised land?
Where are my roots?
Nothing but bloodshed, I see.
Dilapidated rooftops
Evenly sitting on the ground.
And where do I go?
For there are no tracks
There are no footprints.
All have been erased
With the passage of time.
In its place I see cracks
And through them, tears.

Feet freeze for lack of direction.
For lack of hope, for lack of faith.
Where do I take mine?
How do I carry those who
Refuse to move,
Seeing nothing to the horizon.
Eyes shed bloody tears.
Doubt and fear abound
In all directions.
Where is my land?
Where is my rest?

Not yours, not mind,
I hear.

The Lone Astronaut

Ruchi Acharya

In was the farthest of North they had ever been
My dull soul and the insolent me
I'm a stargazer placing my thanks for nights
that turned into blue mornings.
I live in a spacecraft painted in lurid white
with neutral luck—
and I was slowly dying.

The time is frozen with no light
Marvelously planned
I chase into the milky-way galaxy
to bless my spirit and hers by side.
I've floated far away from home
creating a space between trust and rest.

She left in the blink of an eye.
All the hopes and memories, she let   fly.

My luminous mind has been tempered
and my lambent soul is broken
yet I loved,
        I loved
until I was lost in the space
under the myriad lights of flickering stars
all alone—the lone astronaut.

The Best American Essay by Alexander Chee

Alayna Abravanel

What are the main characters (characteristics) of the unholy? My question is, what types of holiness do you have when it comes to becoming a Jew? Something like taking all your thoughts that you may have talked to your professor about in your essay? And try to discuss with your teacher whether you don't have to do the essay if you want to, or you don't want to write your thoughts on your essay for school or in your apartment. What if you don't have the book you already have in your house? Whatever it takes and/or how long it takes for you to finish the book on time. If you're late for your class, then you'll be kicked out of class immediately and you'll never (be allowed to) come to class again.

Hitting the Showers

Thomas J. Misuraca

I pulled off my shirt and caught the sharp odor of my sweaty body. Similar scents filled the locker room as the guys in my gym class prepared for fourth period after a vigorous game of basketball. B.O. was almost pleasant in comparison to the locker room's usual smell of mildew and grimy lockers.

My bare feet stepped over the cold, bumpy tiles and onto the slick, wet floor of the shower room. The water hit my body in a weak, freezing stream. Goose flesh rippled over my skin.

My eyes struggled to avoid looking at my classmates as they stood naked beneath the showers. But I'm drawn to their bodies. Each in different stages of puberty. Some legs sprouted hair, some chests filled out and a few Adam's apples protruded from necks.

And the occasional secret glimpse of other body parts.

A pair of eyes met mine. He motioned toward me, pointing with his soapy finger. "Milo's got a boner!" he exclaimed.

I looked down in disbelief. My own body betrayed me. It felt as if a thousand eyes stared at my nakedness, in every sense of the term. I covered myself and turned away. Laughter echoed through the cave-like shower room.

"Fag!" somebody shouted.

Their insults shot at me like an AR-15.

"His dick's fucking tiny, man!"

"Who's your boyfriend? Martin Walters?"

"I saw them together in the bathroom once. Think they were blowing each other."

"Bet he's thinking about sucking mine, fucking freak."

"He'd choke on mine."

"In your wet dreams."

"Bet he's the girl."

"Even other fags wouldn't want to fuck him."

"Queer boy better not try to kiss me. I'll break his neck."

I closed my eyes. Ignoring them was the only way I'd survive. I pictured myself in the future, far away from these ignorant boys, when it gets better, like so many have promised.

A bar of soap struck the small of my back.

If I survive that long.

Stanfordites

Julie Rico

The lofty minds
of Stanford await,
the dinner table
has been set.

The plates,
the forks,
the spoons,
the glasses,
the napkins
all silent witnesses
to my inquisition.

"How did you get here
sitting with us
at OUR table?
We know he brought you,
but how did you get here?
What do you do?
Where do you live?
Where did you go to college?
Did you really have an art gallery?

                                     Yes, I had 4.

Seldom do Stanfordites
see brown skin
so near them.
My status
is placed there,
on my brown skin.

I can see the calculations
going on in their heads.

"She owns no property,
she has a crummy education
from a public university,
she seemed to accomplish
something with her art galleries,
but how did that happen?
Who did she have…"

My heart sinks,
I want to crawl
under the table.

It is not the being left out.
It is the bias.
It is the reason I am left out,
all of my history erased,
my father's history
my mother's history.
The history of the great indigenous people
I have in my veins
who once tamed this land… their land
I was once the owner here.

I am erased in a few seconds,
I am a pee-on,
I come from pobres,
I have no influence,
I do not belong with them.
They, the cogs of industry,
me, the slave.

It is here,
at the bottom
of the caste
I stay.
They will not
let me leave.

Here I wait,

until they give
me permission
to rise above.
I am in a cell
with shackles placed on me
by America
by white America.

The American Essay by Kathryn Shulz

Alayna Abravanel

Can you please tell me all about writing your essay for college or school assignments and making sure you get to your classroom on time? You don't have to do the essay at the last minute. This is what you should or should not do to your professor or your students, like yelling, cursing, screaming, kicking, biting your hand and your fingers, and last but not least hitting your classmates on school grounds, and dating is against the school policy.

Self Connection

Lois Jackson King

Never the thought of being alienated; in keeping a fixed mind, I am able to be strong, and by encouraging myself, I feel bold enough to conquer my goal.

When and if the feeling of estrangement comes with any degree of power, I'm taking hold of self's inner-man of strength and confidence of generated boldness.

Giving spiritual instruction and directions of "back you go, returning to the hellish foundation of reminders, of much guilt, pain, and shame there is no room for you at this time or any other time."

Thanks, but no thanks; you did once have a space, but thanks to God it was merely a big tempo; but today the welcome mat is no more. I heard a voice say, "Conquer reality." So now with joy, I'm at peace.

Out of Place

Mojdeh Amini

in and out
of place

all Insight me
eternally

deep
|
|
|
|
|
|
|
|

Caving in
Crawling beneath
Cascading
Captivating
Cropping up

Place
is
eternally
Insight/
outside

me

Sun splashing
Its lights

escaping
Non sequitur

Out of Place?

in and out
of places

all Insight me
eternally

deep

|
|
|
|
|
}
|
|

facing
In any way

turning
In any way

still
eternally

insight me
no way to

escape

Onwards 2024

TDM

suffrage, terror, conspiracy
panic—stranded in
isolation etched in one's mind

starting December two thousand one nine
the first case and memory

of Covid comes from far east,

reinforced by memories
threads; the WHO declares we are
in bed, with a Pandemic–

but don't panic, the media begins
assuming; stories crafted
of finely woven silk, iridescent,

bioluminescent, unnerving like in December
2020, there is vaccine authorized for emergency
use, people celebrate instead of

feeling aloof, however,
like in nature, Covid changed
with various patterns

without definition, like fresh
snowflakes forming; quizzically
in all directions, so in December

2021 Omicron
was identified—a name,
to remember 'O'

though the terror, conspiracy,
panic subsided, a web
of connections lingers, where

our continued suffering
brings the strings together; in—
at the knot or in between lines

Taylor Swift

Alayna Abravanel

Tomorrow is the day to see a movie of a female singer, Taylor Swift, and the girls; and that is why Taylor Swift is awesome and she's the country singer of the day. And I would like to give a round of applause to the one and only Taylor Swift, and her band?

Eclipse by Stephanie Meyer

Alayna Abravanel

Part: 1

The Twilight book is about when Bella and Jacob the Werewolf defeated the vampires. And going out when it comes to fighting the enemies and sometimes they like to talk about fighting vampires. They loved going to the library to read books and hanging out at Barnes and Noble to buy some romance books for Bella's birthday. And also going to the book sale to buy used books and new books.

Part: 2

So Jacob the Werewolf is trying to save Bella and the kids. And he was making them breakfast and they were making themselves some coffee with sugar and creamer, and maybe making some lunch as well.

Part: 3

What is Team Jacob doing to the poor werewolf? Is he trying to be safe and take good care of the kids? And making something like an iced latte or making them other beverages to make them feel better?

(2)^2 cents for Outliers

TDM

when your blood doesn't feel like your blood,
let them speak—while you practice;

    one—in mind,
        two—in breath,
            three—being free,

               and then
                    you respond
                       with Silence…

when you feel inept in place,
surrounded amongst strangers—muster courage;

    one—in smile,
        two—in interest,
            three—lean; in camaraderie,

             maybe
               you feel like being
                  in a new you; then…

when all else fails from depress,
a doom and gloom in fallback—the end;

    one—in prayer,
        two—in constitution
            three—is where light you'll see,

             be in the present
               in the moment
                  is to be alive…

when in doubt, through feelings of alienation,
dive in—lead without fear;

      one—in cognition,
          two—in body,
              three—in soul,

                    staying
                        the
                              uncharted course…

A Blue Day in a Blue Bathroom

Claudia Santos

Shards of Beauty

Julie Rico

My world once held hands with love.
I held tightly onto the strings of life,
knotting them together
one by one.

I climbed the knots I made,
till my life was made,
then unmade, then made again.

A collage of kindness
began to appear,
a tapestry of beauty
was everywhere.

One day a summer day,
a sunny lovely day,
a sudden chill
fell upon my land.

Vicious strangers appeared
replacing love with laws
and tenderness with terror.

The strangers say,
we are the owners,
they say my land is their land.
They enacted laws,
built court houses,
hired police,

"to ensure the peace."

My spirit now wilts
in the heat of the sun.
The trees once bore green olives,

they healed me.
Now their leaves are
covered in soot.

See, look behind me
a maze of imprisoned souls.
See, look beside me,
we line the streets.
See, look ahead of me
my world of love

                is filled with hate.

Shards of beauty
lie beneath
my feet.

Tells of Truth

Lois Jackson King

You speak of fairness and truth; I'm with you.
The wrong way shall be given what to do.

Mercy me, you seem to be on the right track.
You are speaking with a great tongue.

What you are saying is powerful and weighs a ton.
Strong and loud; to hear more, to you, I will run.

Have I misunderstood the appropriate meaning?
Your fairness is self-exhortation over the Right Wing.

The Constitution of The United States says it "All."
All "Humanity" is in the "Liberty." All are entitled.

Your speaking power is the weight on people of color's necks.
Those not following your lead, their lives you desire to wreck.

Strong for all of the wrong reasons; forsaking truth for lies.
Caught up in your woven schemes, a web, trapped like a fly.

Ni de función ni de quince

Sanjui

Caminando voy en duelo
Como pidiendo un tratado
Al realista del derecho
Al rango del izquierdo

Mi dolor que pesa
cae a cada lado
Sin relación de seguir el cliente
Del prematuro baile sin son ni pobreza

Al lado setenta, el viento factura
consuelo mi cabello sin droga
Tal vez interrumpiendo la frecuencia
De quien lo alivie en su lugar

Ay de mí, ¡Qué preocupación!
Aspirante al plomo que alivia,
Que soy de reproche o de excluir,
Que bravo quien reclame,
Mis piscinas, mis dibujos, mis pretextos.

Con la mirada preferida
Hacia el ángel
Y un bordo hondo
Captaré al mar mis ilusiones
Y enamoraré mi alma de la vejez.

Emotional Pain

Lois Jackson King

Yes, kicked all around
With so many kicks all over me
I'm still alive and not in the ground
Misplaced, without a doubt
Voicing my thoughts, I be tossed about
I'm misplaced; and so is my voice
Where is the voice; can't make that choice
Voice being whipped and kicked around
Misplaced and dare to make a sound
Depression is not where I am bound
In many places my face is as a clown
Shunned, and the inner me full of frowns
Being ignored for whatever reason
Harm is being done on today's social media
It shouldn't matter, ethnic history, old or young
Purposefully misplaced by other's rejection, it's no fun

Las Palmas

Tauwan Patterson

These houses are so big
Their lawns never-ending
So California

I lived in a house once
I had a home
Now,

I wander
As if on some magic carpet ride
To where?—I don't know

Though I prefer some place steady, fixed
Like these palatial mansions eyeing me in silence
As I admire their wares, also in silence,

Plotting, scheming (or desperately needing to)
All the while thinking:
I wanna go home.

Just haven't found it yet.

Gordian Knot

Zelda Harrison

Here I am
Bound by your Rules
and Norms, your Ponzi
Pyramid of
Knowledge, Notions of Exclusivity,
Treadmills of Acquisition
Esoteric Codes of Conduct
that Mutate,
Goal Posts that keep Shifting…

Here. I. Am.
Wrapped and Warped,
Hamstrung, but
Quietly stoking the glimmering
Consciousness of
your Transience & Frailty,
chinks in the
Mesh of edifices
erected to Maintain,
Assuage, Ascertain
Your Perch.

You say:
"Chin up, Strap up!
It's all so simple,
one step forward,
two steps back!"

Indeed. Occam Be Praised!

So simple…
I take one step forward,
And Slice.

Kendrick Van Gogh

Tauwan Patterson

hair like Sideshow
Bob plus height, too
stalking the halls like a Messiah
draped in mystery's cloak
urbana's very own dark matter
america's wasted youth
top dawg entertainment, blessED
wordsmith
disjointed
mind movement rapid like a lotto ball machine
KING KUNTA
vibe seeker
tainted wonder
on that Hendrix
dialogue momentous guitarl
to a flame burned
by the fire

Black Tar Friends

Julie Rico

The dread I feel
is now incessant
gloom.

You are
the cause,
the head,
that rattles with hate.

I step on the stones,
you laid for me,
your hidden vicious deeds
did unveil,
the road you laid
so I might fail.

Hark now angels
hear me,
surround me
with safety.
Give me a path
to tread that is easy.

You, the white one,
the chosen one,
skip on.
My ruinous fate prevails.

In vain, I toil,
in vain, I dream,
in vain I live.

I crawl
from my pit of darkness,
my bloody knees scraped deep.

Your icy breath,
a thick fog,
cover acts unknown.

I lift and turn my head,
to see the world.
Then I am knocked down
to the place of hate.
My brown eyes
do meet the sky above,
a glimpse of beauty,
of calm of love.

Come close,
white one
Nemesis has
a gift for you.

We are
black tar friends.
It is our fate.

Fear

Mojdeh Amini

When shadow of fear
is greater than
fear itself

When fear runs
Into us with no fears

When fear coexists inside us
in thousands of ways

without a single way
to exit

When fear is so
fearless

shifted away
From inside to the outside

acierta buscar espacio

River

  bailarín planetas
   hostilidad huecos
    de motas de mota de mota sorprendente polvo
temperatura pollos en el sol
hay soles desviando la luna
hay 'hay' en el rencor
   granosa nada realismo nadir

                proporción
               indicación,
                  educación:
   pon el pie campeón guantes de
  vacío   proporcionar   vacilante
mi dulce cuenta, instrucción de los universos

be right in searching space

River

   dancer planets
    hostility voids
      of motes of mote of mote surprising dust
temperature chickens in the sun
there are suns diverting the moon
there is "there is" in the rancor
    grainy nothing(swims) realism nadir

                      proportion
                      indication
                         education:
    put your champion foot gloves of
    empty   to provide   vacillating
my sweet story, instructions of the universes

a buscar espacio

River

  de planetas
   de huecos
    de motas de mota de mota del polvo
hay pollos en el sol
hay soles en la luna
hay 'hay' en el hay
   granosa nada al nadir

              pinchazos,
             inverosímiles,
               agujeros:
    pon el pie en guantes de
   vacía   vacilidad   vacilante
mi dulce cuenta, hije de los universos

on searching space

River

  of planets
  of voids
   of motes of mote of mote from the dust
there are chickens in the sun
there are suns in the moon
There is "there is" in the there is
   grainy nothing(swims) at(to) the nadir

                pricks
               unreal,
                 holes
   put your foot in gloves of
  empty   vacillation   vacillating
my sweet telling, child of the universes

String Theory

Luz Donis

Tiny strings
humming, stitching
life on a loom
handed down

Bright patterns embedded
on fabric threaded
colors in fleeces
　　　in folds
　　　in creases

Dramatic knots
punctuate
seams
crinkle and crumple
wrinkle and ruffle
seem
to negate

Some tied loose
unravel flaws
others hold tight
secrets
unresolved

Never mere
gossamer
ethereal
strings
stringing us along

Wizard

Ruchi Acharya

The heart was bestowed to me from the outer space
I always carry the burden of the past earthen lovers
who grew old together in the midst of corn fields,
who sunbathed in summer and read the books dearly.

In the year three thousand twenty-three,
Reality warps, unasked; into the smoke we breathe
Enchantment of darkness, unfold the Jupiter's moonbeams
beneath the moon's eldritch glow, I behold—
all my secrets, amulets, lies, potions, and poisoned keys.

The heavens summon the birds who lost their flight.
The ancients have passed their powers;
I can feel in my heart, the mass destruction; weaponised.
All the sunflowers have died and lovers lost lovers.
Knowledge becomes a fragment of Life's twilight.

To act as the protector of the realm is not a cup of tea,
I am an old wizard living in a shack with sorcery,
Receiving signals from the galaxy.
Is it a trap from the outer world's human beings
Or my lovers whom I never met or seen?

negro swan

Tauwan Patterson

for devonte

bring hope when you come around.
still smile when you come around.

i feel seen.

he is i, and i am him!

am given a reminder that i belong.

with you, i feel this and we connect.
brotha to brotha, man to man,
as we are.

no one wants to be the odd man out at times, so we just be.

you just be.

negro swan, breaking the act.

relax your hair. tuck your shirt. put your glasses on…

as you are.
wrapped in sumptuous melanin,
all the way up.

nappy wonder.

your skin's a flag that shines for us all.
the charcoal babies,
the brothas feelin' themselves,
those whose internal resolution is to do too much,
because,

why would you want to do the least?…

so you don't.
and you break the act.

dreamy,

crushed velvet,
funk laced.
swathed in black excellence,

lifting every voice to sing and be seen;
be reminded that you belong.

nappy wonder.

negro swan.

* *negro swan contains lines and dialogue from the Blood Orange
tracks "Saint", "Hope", "Jewelry", and "Charcoal Baby".*

Root of It All

Lois Jackson King

To Be or Not to Be
What shall I see
Knots overshadow me

Is all life woven this way
I truly want to go but
I am compelled to say

What is the woven factor
Dusty-me, now a fleshly character
Knotting together does it matter

No sirree; not man-made for sure
But flesh and blood that's pure
Colonizing, but where's the cure

This here is your new approach
Causing many of us to revoke
A true displacement which makes to stoke

Pain to our already broken heart
Doom cutting our tradition short
Lack of knowledge made it hard to start

What may be common to you, we say poop
Programs putting my spirit to a great stoop
Confusion and mind-blowing proofs

The feeling of being shut out and misplaced
Knowing not what to do in making me hide my face
Out of my "Native" comfort zone as if out in space

Many around and yet I feel so all alone
When will I connect the knots and hear a tone
Of which I have been pulled apart

The chain or string of networking the style
Technology knotting and we smile
Part of the common thread, a great file

Knotting together, come with sweat
Making life events; others giving birth
Textile just the new birth to earth

Bring forth different and unique textile produce
Yes, we are the symbolic helpers to reduce
Together is the pattern to textile "Root"

Farmland

Ruchi Acharya

You lay back on a hay bale, looking up
The golden rays shining down,
you're sulking in your soul
Stand up and take a look around
Feel the feels, the vibrations
the moths' buzz, cuckoos' frequencies surround

Watch the harvesters work, scythes in tune
Blood and sweat dripping
under straw hats strewn
Sky can heal the tethered hearts
People can be false, dragonflies surreal
Fill your soul's trenches with the sun, moon and earth.

Don't be tied down by thoughts that so sigh
and watch the sands of time slip away
Listen to your body,
grow your mind; let your farmland shine
Mud and swine, grape yard vines smelling a fine wine.

Let Me Go Home

Sanjui

This land is not my land.
I must return to where the trees abound
Where their colors change with time
Fall, spring, summer, winter.

I want to be known by everyone I meet in the street.
Where a smile is a given
And a handshake is a must.

I must return to where memories bind Us
to our roots in the house that was once ours.

I cannot wait to feel the pouring of rain.
Or see the dancing in the sky in a stormy night,
Where the sound of thunder is felt down deep in my heart.

I, Desert, must not remain in this dry land,
Where the trees don't find favor in growing,
And the desperate land cries,
For a single drop of rain.

I must go Home!

SUNSET BLVD.

Tauwan Patterson

We first locked eyes next to the Viper Room,across from the Whisky.
        I gave the nod,

he gave no response. My eyes quickly darted elsewhere, focusing
        on anything—the tiny bottle of clear booze in his hands
        /his fit/

the interior of the liquor store he was exiting—to squash
        the awkwardness,
briefly mourn the Black male camaraderie now lost. Turning right

heading south, here we were again, crossing paths. God
must be trying to tell me something came across

unsaid in the urgency of his tone, his quest
to now gain my undivided attention

                        Man, look.
                        I'm out here

                        from New Jersey.
                        Five dollars to my name.

                        I'm trying… I mean
                        I have Cash App.

                        But I only have
                        Five dollars… Crazy

                        shit man.
                        I'm out here.

                        Girl had me
                        believing she was pregnant.

I stood there rapt, scanning his face, ashamed
for wondering if—game recognize game—

the acne all over his mug was a product of a hard knock life.
His plea continued.

I sang the standard Sorry man,
no cash.

He followed up with a quick You got Cash App?
Apple Pay?...

Another sea of no's
breaking the chain.

No anger in his voice, he shouted
I'MMA BE AIGHT THO! from the middle of the street.

I turned around, wanting to acknowledge his pending come up
with a head nod, a non verbal fa sho. That's what's up.

But he was gone. Lost again
to the streets like a rocket in flight.

Exit

Thomas J. Misuraca

"You're not from around here, are you?" A girl approached Dean as he gassed up his car at a Mobile station off Interstate 5.

She tried to make herself look older with her wavy blonde hair trickling down to her shoulders, over-applied make-up, tight jeans hugging her waist, and a red t-shirt exposing her thin, pale stomach. But Dean could see the youthfulness in her face.

"Nope," Dean replied and turned his attention to cleaning the dead bugs off his windshield. *She's gonna hit me up to buy her cigarettes*, Dean thought.

"Where're you headed?" The girl stood next to his car as he finished cleaning his windows.

"North."

"Can you take me with you?"

This evoked a surprised laugh from Dean. "You don't even know where I'm going."

"Yes I do," she replied. "North."

Dean chuckled as he replaced the squeegee, avoiding direct eye contact with the girl.

"I just want to get as far away from here as possible," she said.

"Aren't you a little young to be wandering so far?"

"I'm old enough."

"What about your parents?"

"What about them?"

"Won't they be concerned about you traveling so far away with a strange man?"

"I've traveled even further with stranger men," she said nonchalantly. "And they never heard about it. Besides, they don't live around here."

"I think you're lying."

The girl shifted uncomfortably.

"What's really going on?"

"I need to get out of here. This place is so boring. Just… look around."

Dean did. A bland, uninspiring small town spread around him. The color had long ago washed out of the place, if there ever was any. The restaurants and convenience stores on this exit appeared run down to the point of abandoned. He couldn't imagine living here. "Why're you asking me?"

"Because you look like a nice guy."

"I am a nice guy," Dean said with a grin. "Too nice to take a young girl away from her family."

"If you don't take me, I'm sure somebody else will. Lots of people come through here. Maybe I'll ask that guy there." She motioned towards a man filling up at the other end of the station. He wore thick glasses and had dark, greasy hair styled with an obvious combover. Dean got the creepy vibe from him immediately. There was no telling what a guy like that would do to a girl if he had her alone on an empty road. "So whadaya say?" the girl pressed.

Without a word, Dean returned the nozzle to the pump and moved to his door. "C'mon," he said. "I'm leaving."

The girl climbed into the passenger seat.

"What's your name?" he asked.

"Judy."

"Nice to meet you Judy, I'm Dean."

"Hi, Dean." He started the car and put it in drive. "Last chance to change your mind."

"Let's roll, Mr. Nice Guy."

Dean hoped he would still be Mr. Nice Guy when he got her alone on the empty road.

blood orange

Tauwan Patterson

Damn near six feet tall, he
was a peer. I could see it

in his face as I glanced at him
quickly, then away, like the rest

around me. We didn't want any trouble,
and neither did he.

He boarded the train shirtless,
barefoot, threadbare gray sweats,

clutching a lighter, his manhood, jellybeans
bright and multi-colored; A rainbow

in the palm of the thunderstorm that was he
standing out like a Negro Swan, arriving

as I pressed play on Devonte's album of the same name, pacing,
frantic. With us, but alone.

Janet Mock's voice preached, stressing
the importance of family, community,

the building of our systems of stability.
As he paced and screamed and terrified some, many of us

silently prayed that he keep himself to himself.
This Negro Swan. In desperate need of family.

In desperate need of community. In desperate need of anything
other than oddity status.

* "Negro Swan" is the fourth studio album by Devonte Hynes aka
Blood Orange. The album contains spoken word interludes from
Janet Mock, a Writer, Director, and Transgender Rights Activist.

Gift of Belonging

Sanjui

Come one, come all!
The gift you have been waiting for!
It is what every child desires
And every parent deserves
It will relieve every inch of your nerves
For this will favor your head.

Come one, come all!
Mario Kart?
Donkey Kong?
Princess and Demons?
Not quite, just another delight.

Time to take off the stress
Keep your child enchanted

Get the latest gadget.
Not a phone, not a tablet
The ultimate and only handheld
So they can feel
like they really belong,
Like they have friends
And solitude is no more!

Give them the gift of belonging.
Where they enter into a world
Of possibly no return
Where their vision may find distortion
And their world will begin to close in.

Get them to push every buttonl
Fire many rounds everywhere
Spend their days feeling "joy"
Giving away their soul.

Come one, come all!
Let your child begin to belong
Let your child begin to get lost.
Bluelight special: One per soul!

INDIAN LAND STOLEN

GET A HOME OF YOUR OWN!

PERFECT LAND

WITHIN OUR BOUNDARIES

FINE LANDS IN THE WEST

PASSED DOWN FROM GENERATION TO GENERATION OF NATIVE AMERICANS

IN 1910 THE DEPARTMENT OF THE INTERIOR STOLE UNDER FALSE PRETENSES INDIAN LAND AS FOLLOWS:

Location.	Acres.	Average Price per Acre.	Location.	Acres.	Average Price per Acre.
Colorado	5,211.21	$7.27	Oklahoma	34,664.00	$19.14
Idaho	17,013.00	24.85	Oregon	1,020.00	15.43
Kansas	1,684.50	33.45	South Dakota	120,445.00	16.53
Montana	11,034.00	9.86	Washington	4,879.00	41.37
Nebraska	5,641.00	36.65	Wisconsin	1,069.00	17.00
North Dakota	22,610.70	9.93	Wyoming	865.00	20.64

FOR THE YEAR 1911 IT IS ESTIMATED THAT 350,000 ACRES WILL BE PAINFULLY STOLEN AND MISUSED

For information as to the character of the land, ask the Natives!

The following places, Do Not represent Us!

CALIFORNIA:
Hoopa.
COLORADO:
Ignacio.
IDAHO:
Lapwai.
KANSAS:
Horton.
Nadeau.

MINNESOTA:
Onigum.
MONTANA:
Crow Agency.
NEBRASKA:
Macy.
Santee.
Winnebago.

NORTH DAKOTA:
Fort Totten.
Fort Yates.
OKLAHOMA:
Anadarko.
Cantonment.
Colony.
Darlington.
Muskogee,
Pawnee.

OKLAHOMA—Con.
Sac and Fox Agency.
Shawnee.
Wyandotte.
OREGON:
Klamath Agency.
Pendleton.
Roseburg.
Siletz.

SOUTH DAKOTA:
Cheyenne Agency.
Crow Creek.
Greenwood.
Lower Brule.
Pine Ridge.
Rosebud.
Sisseton.

WASHINGTON:
Fort Simcoe.
Fort Spokane.
Tekoa.
Tulalip.
WISCONSIN:
Oneida.

WALTER L. FISHER,
Secretary of the Interior.

ROBERT G. VALENTINE,
Commissioner of Indian Affairs.

WhiteWash By: Abraham Jaramillo

Hear Me Out Judge Elmer Dundy

Abraham Jaramillo

In the early morning hours dragging feet
sometimes woke me up, the sound
of my dad going to the restroom, not an empty house

A busy house, my two nephews running around,
bouncing up and down, surprising
grandma by knowing the password
of a tablet with a broken screen

A somewhat safe neighborhood,
a shooting we still remember and
tools stolen in the middle of the night,
is all the bad light, I can give to my suburban Land

Busy life, I have worked in this neighborhood
ever since I came here, not a native,
but definitely in the making,
I still hung with my friends from high school,
Poke a friend, we didn't know his real name
until a girl asked for Angel,
Chileno,
        Panama,
                Peru,

yeah not the most creative nicknames, but we loved soccer
a sport that connected us all, we all moved around,
around the same town, or somewhat,

and somehow,

I was dragged out of my home, with nothing,
only with what I could carry with me,

We walked and we walked,
        We walked and we walked,
                We walked and we walked,

I still remember a big guy, looking like
a Standing bear, with an extinguishing stare
for the march was long, insufferable,
arduous, cruel, long...

Now, I found myself in a place
with not a single face to call a friend
no more soccer games to play,
no kids playing around, for my nephews
never made it here,
                remember,
insufferable, arduous, cruel, long... walk

So hear me out,

I have no love for this new Land as
I have no love for the scorching sun
or the green lawns of a golf course,
I am here in front of a Man
who's Given power has the force
to end this insufferable syndrome   of colonial displacement
and give me Home, my Home back,
and let me go   back.

55

Out of *Offense*

Abraham Jaramillo

I want to be more than an accent **surprise**
amongst the **tissue** natives

I want to feel part of the **barrier** heard
and feel the **compartment** love

I am tired of the **appoint** stares
as if all but me were **institution** the same

I am unique and not a **brainstorm** ashamed,
but not in any **miscarriage** of form, out of place.

Fibers

Abraham Jaramillo

Strong ancient fibers try to bend my
voice **"you are a rug"** they tell me

And so, my fiber fights with
every fiber to become a
rock concert jacket made
to fit the right soul

Orange and red strings twist
and turn fibers on
fire burst onto a field of
dead black, strings which only
rejoice in the night

Knots form in my throat and yet
I speak my mind for
a string that knows where
it wants to go
can't be bend and forever Rock and Roll…!

About the Authors
.... Sobre los autores

Mojdeh Amini

As a bilingual, I enjoy writing poems and prose in English. I love our Conchas y Café Zine poetic and artistic community, a virtual place to learn, to share, and grow.

Sanjui

Sanjuanita is a teacher at LAUSD. She has 4 kids, a beautiful granddaughter and one more coming soon. She also has a cute dog name OREO. She loves to read and write. Her passion is writing poetry.

Ruchi Acharya

Ruchi Acharya, hailing from India, is a distinguished English Laureate. Over the past two years, she has gained immense recognition for her remarkable publications, with her works appearing in more than 100 renowned platforms.

Alayna Abravanel

Alayna Abravanel joined our Conchas y Café workshop series after participating in our *Journal of My Life* series offered in partnership with the Los Angeles Public Library. Alayna tries to express herself in as many was as she can.

Tomas J. Misuraca

Tom Misuraca is the author of over 130 published short stories and two novels. His story, *Giving Up The Ghosts*, was published in *Constellations Journal*, and nominated for a Pushcart Prize in 2021. His work has recently appeared in *voidspace*, *The Cafe Irreal* and *Speakeasy Mag*. | www.tommiz.com | Instagram: @tmisuraca | facebook.com/tom.misuraca/

Julie Rico

Once an acclaimed art gallery owner in Los Angeles and Santa

Monica, Julie Rico sat on the board of the Bilingual Foundation of the Arts. She was the executive producer of the LAARTSFEST. Julie managed the Mean Art Tent of the 1995 US Lollapalooza Tour, a curated traveling exhibition. l www.juliericogallery.com

Lois Jackson King
A retired educator with degrees in Social Behavior, Christian Education and Christian Counseling as well as an Ordained Minister of the Gospel. Mother of 4, a grandmother of 10, a great-grandmother of 11, and one great-great-granddaughter.

T.D.M.
An author with a passion for creating human experiences, T.D.M is a lifelong designer, creator and photographer exploring all forms of creative expression hoping to make a positive impact in the world.

Claudia Santos
Claudia Santos (@claudiaexcaret) is a Mexican English Major, poet, interpreter, translator, and cultural gestor. She has been published in the digital magazine *Fleas on the Dog*, the printed anthology *Boundless 2022*, the Spanish magazines *Punto de partida*, *Blog Libropolis*, *Letralia*, *La poesía Alcanza*, etc. l linktr.ee/claudiaexcaret

Tauwan Patterson
Hailing from South Central, Los Angeles, Tauwan Patterson is a Black + Queer Poet & recent graduate of the MFA Creative Writing Program at Queens University of Charlotte, North Carolina.

Zelda Harrison
Zelda Harrison is a cross-cultural creature who is constantly seeking new horizons of worlds within words. I use poetry to play with words I never get to use in real life, to breathe and feel anew.

River
River (They/them) writes as a way to puzzle the world into and out of place. With a habit to string different shapes, themes, containers, like holiday lights out of season, their work ranges

from soothing to tumultuous and they never quite know what they are going to get.

Luz Donis

Luz is a second generation Guatemalan, raised in Boyle Heights. She trained and worked as a nurse for L.A. County and L.A. Unified. She is currently immersed in Vipassana insight meditation, ceramics, and being a grandma.

Abraham Jaramillo

Planet Earth Artist, bound to create art that reflects nature, a range of human emotions, and a multitude of other topics using different types of media, such as poetry, photography, painting, etc. To discover more of his madness, follow him on his Instagram (@abraham_photoworld), or his website www.a0jphotoworld.com.

About the Conchas y Café program

Conchas y Café is a 15-week workshop series for adults, focusing exclusively on creative writing, literacy, and illustration. Participants have the opportunity to work with volunteer writers and artists on developing artwork that will be published and presented in a biannual zine and public reading.

For more information, locations, and dates for upcoming Conchas y Café workshops, contact us by email at *info@DSTLArts.org*.

Acerca el programa Conchas y Café

Conchas y Café es un taller de 15 semanas para adultos, especializando en escritura, literatura, y dibujo. Participantes tienen la oportunidad de trabajar con escritores y artistas voluntarios en el desarrollo de obras de arte que serán publicados y presentados en publicaciones bianuales y lecturas públicas.

Para más información, localidades, y fechas de próximos talleres de Conchas y Café, contáctenos por correo electronico al *info@DSTLArts.org*.

This program is supported in part by:

Conchas y Café Zine
Vol. VIII, Issue 3

Pen & Tongue
Pluma y Lengua

a DSTL arts publication

Pen & Tongue: Conchas y Café Zine; Vol. 8, Issue 3
available now at DSTLArts.org/shop

This publication was produced by DSTL Arts.

DSTL Arts is a nonprofit arts mentorship organization that inspires, teaches, and hires emerging artists from underserved communities.

To learn more about DSTL Arts, visit online at:
DSTLArts.org
@DSTLArts